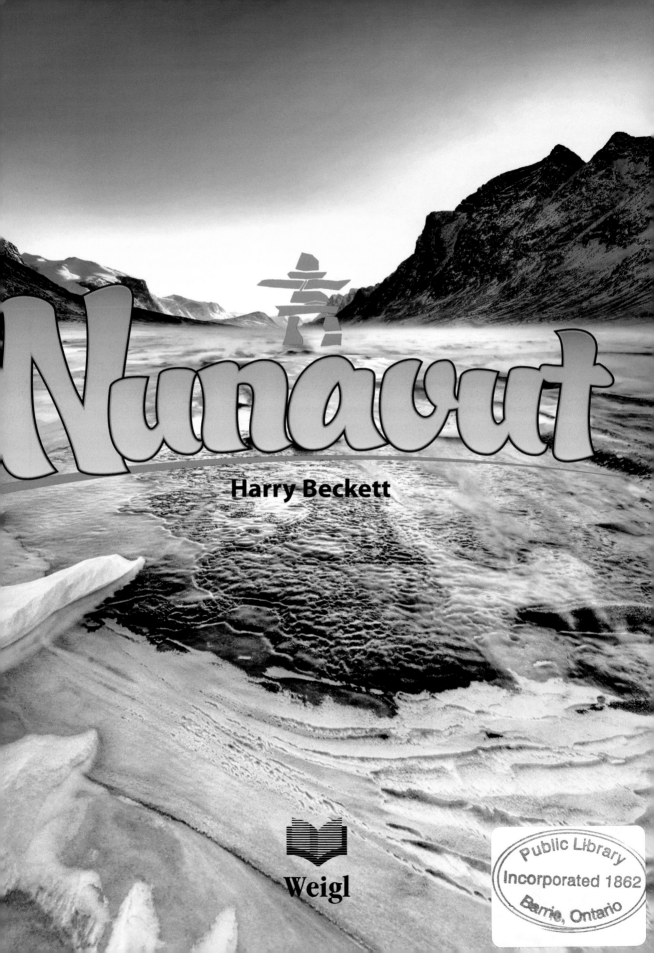

Nunavut

Harry Beckett

Weigl

Published by Weigl Educational Publishers Limited
6325 – 10 Street SE
Calgary, Alberta, Canada
T2H 2Z9

Website: www.weigl.ca

Library and Archives Canada Cataloguing in Publication
Beckett, Harry, 1936-, author
        Nunavut / Harry Beckett.
(Provinces)
Issued in print and electronic formats.
ISBN 978-1-4872-0269-9 (bound).--ISBN 978-1-4872-0270-5 (pbk.).--
ISBN 978-1-4872-0271-2 (ebook)
        1. Nunavut--Juvenile literature. I. Title.
FC4311.2.B433 2015   j971.9'5   C2015-900972-3
                                               C2015-900973-1

Printed in the United States of America in Brainerd, Minnesota
1 2 3 4 5 6 7 8 9 0 19 18 17 16 15

082015
100815

We acknowledge the financial support of the Government of Canada through
the Canada Book Fund for our publishing activities.

Project Coordinator: Heather Kissock
Designer: Terry Paulhus

CONTENTS

Eye on Nunavut

Before April 1999, Nunavut was part of the Northwest Territories. Since then, it has become a territory of its own. Nunavut is the largest of all the provinces and territories, at about one-fifth of Canada's area. To the West are the Inuvik and Fort Smith regions. Manitoba, Hudson Bay, and Quebec border it to the south. Baffin Bay and the Labrador Sea border it to the east.

During the last Ice Age, glaciers up to 5 kilometres thick moved across Nunavut. They scraped the rock bare and then retreated. Icecaps 2 kilometres thick still cover much of Ellesmere Island and parts of Devon and Baffin Islands.

Travelling in Nunavut

Nunavut covers almost 2 million square kilometres, and is 2,400 kilometres at its widest. Due to the territory's rugged terrain, its huge area, and the limited number of people who travel in the North, there are no railways in Nunavut. Outside the towns, there are only about 21 kilometres of road on Baffin Island.

Boat travel is another mode of transportation, but it is limited by the ice that covers much of the water. However, freezing weather can be helpful to other modes of transportation. People use snowmobiles to get around when the land is snow covered and the waterways are frozen.

In some places, glaciers left behind ridges of gravel, called eskers.

GEOGRAPHY

Nunavut sits almost entirely above the **Arctic tree line**.

ECONOMY

Mining makes up almost **35%** of Nunavut's **economy**.

HISTORY

Scientists believe that **Vikings** visited Baffin Island **1000 years ago**.

CULTURE

Nunavut has the **youngest** median age, **23.5 years**, out of all the provinces and territories.

Sites and Symbols

Nunavut has its own unique identity. It uses a variety of symbols to represent this identity to Canada and the world. These symbols showcase the people, history, culture, and natural beauty of the province.

Entered Confederation:
April 1, 1999
Capital: Iqaluit
Area: 2,093,190 sq. km
Population: 31,906

What's in a Name?

Nunavut comes from the Inuktitut **dialect** of the Eastern Arctic Inuit. It translates to "our land." This is significant to Nunavut's creation. The struggle to establish an Inuit territory began in 1976. It was not until 1992 that the Inuit and Canada's federal government could agree on all issues. A land claim agreement was signed in 1993 and Nunavut became an official territory in 1999. This agreement gave the Inuit control over 351,000 square kilometres of Nunavut.

Nunavut's Legislative Building incorporates the idea of the Inuit Qaggip, or meeting place.

The Provincial Coat of Arms

Nunavut's coat of arms features many Inuit symbols. The shield is blue and gold, which represents the sea and the sky. Within the shield are an **inukshuk** and qulliq, a stone lap symbolizing the Inuit family. The Sun tracks across the top third of the shield, with the North Star above it. An igloo sits on the top, and on either side are a caribou and a **narwhal**, all necessities to traditional Inuit life. The motto across the bottom reads *Nunavut Sanginivut*, Inuktitut for "Our land, our strength."

Nunavut's Official Flag

Nunavut's official flag features four colours, all representing a part of the territory's identity. The flag is half white, symbolising the Arctic land, and half yellow, symbolizing the sky. The blue star stands for both the sea and the Niqirtsituk, or North Star, a key part of navigation for the Inuit. The inukshuk dividing the yellow and white halves is red, a reference to Canada.

Nunavut Map

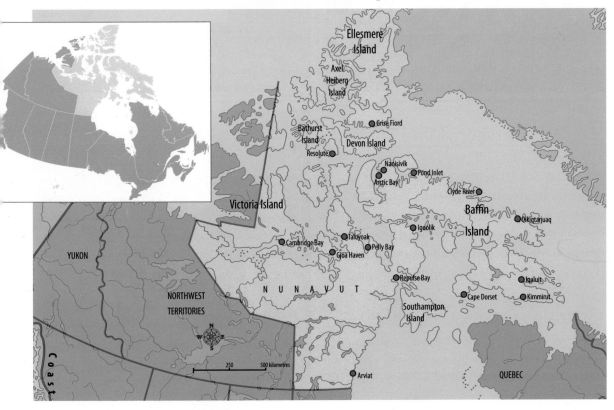

Nunavut's Flower Emblem

The purple saxifrage was adopted as Nunavut's official flower in May 2000. The flower is one of the first to bloom in the Arctic spring and is therefore a welcome sight for northerners. Its broad, purple petals stand in stark contrast to the harsh white of the Arctic. Tea made from the petal and stems can help relieve gastric problems.

Nunavut's Territorial Bird

The rock ptarmigan is Nunavut's official bird and is a true bird of the Arctic. Whereas other birds fly south for the winter, rock ptarmigans make their home in the Arctic year round. Between seasons, their plumage changes colour. In winter, they are all white, blending in with the snow. In the spring and summer, they have a more mottled colour, with white, brown, and grey feathers. Their changing plumage colour helps the ptarmigan hide from predators.

The Territorial Animal

Nunavut's official animal is the Canadian Inuit Dog, or quimmiq. It is considered one of the oldest **pure breeds** in the world and has been in the Canadian Arctic for an estimated 4,000 years. This dog is beloved by the Inuit, helping them travel long distances by pulling sleds. In the past, the quimmiq helped the Inuit hunt by finding seal breathing holes in the ice, and protected them from muskox and polar bears.

Official Symbol

Nunavut chose the inukshuk as its territorial symbol. These rock formations have the rough shape of a human. The inukshuk is integral to Inuit identity. It can help point the way along travel routes, mark sacred sites, and act as centres of communication.

Territorial Licence Plate

The Nunavut licence plate features an inukshuk in the design, along with 25 stars, a polar bear, and the northern lights. The stars represent each of the 25 communities in Nunavut.

LAND AND CLIMATE

Nunavut's landscape is a mixture of mountains, fjords, lakes, and **tundra**. The mainland and Baffin Island are part of the **Canadian Shield**. Much of the territory's land was shaped by glaciers. The ice sheets reached the Arctic Ocean coastline, creating deep valleys and fjords.

On Axel Heiberg Island, Baffin Island, and the eastern part of Ellesmere Island, mountains range from 1,500 to 2,000 metres in height. The rest of Nunavut is a high, flat plateau gashed by ravines and covered in lakes, **muskeg**, and swamps. The islands to the west are low.

Most of Nunavut's many rivers are on the mainland. Since the land is low-lying and irregular, the rivers often widen out to form lakes. The biggest lake on the mainland is Dubawnt Lake. Most of the rivers on Baffin Island are on the west side. These rivers are short because the sea is never very far away. Nunavut's two largest lakes, Nettilling and Amadjuak, are on Baffin Island. Ellesmere Island also boasts large lakes. Lake Hazen is 72 km long and nearly 10 km wide. It is the largest lake in the area.

Nunavut's ground is frozen for most of the year, which is an indication of how cold the territory can get. Winters in Nunavut are very long and cold. Daily January temperatures average −20° Celsius on south Baffin Island and about −37° C on north Ellesmere Island. Nunavut's short summers can average 21° C, and for a short time, flowers can bloom. However, cold prevails, and it is possible to build igloos by November.

February, 1979, was the **coldest** month ever recorded in North America. Eureka, in what is now Nunuvut, had an average temperature of **-47.8° C.**

Most of Nunavut's gold comes from the Meadowbank mine.

NATURAL RESOURCES

The Canadian Shield contains many minerals, but finding and exploiting them in such a remote place as Nunavut is difficult. The expense of transportation and the freezing weather are big challenges to the mining industry. The lead and zinc mines of Nanisivik and Polaris are almost always icebound. Only in summer can ships bring in supplies and carry the ore out.

Exploration in Nunavut has shown that it has rich deposits in gold, uranium, and iron. There have been talks between Nunavut and the federal government to further explore and mine these resources. This would bring an increase in revenue to Nunavut and make it less dependent on the federal government.

Mining activities began in the barren lands along the Thelon River after diamonds were discovered there. Nunavut's first diamond mine, Jericho, opened in 2006. Although it closed in 2008, the potential for mining diamonds remains.

Nunavut also has large oil and gas deposits in the northern Arctic Ocean. These reserves can only be developed when world oil prices make it possible. Otherwise, the expense of drilling in this area is much too great.

Most of Canada's polar bear population lives in Nunavut.

PLANTS AND ANIMALS

Nunavut's infertile, shallow soil is frozen all winter, making life difficult for plants. The few plants that live in the territory survive the bitter winters and summers by crowding together. They find shelter in rock crevices or by lying flat to the ground. Lichens and mosses, with some spindly bushes, cover the tundra.

About 200 species of flowers, including dandelions and buttercups, survive to bloom in the long hours of summer sunlight. People and animals take advantage of the blossoming plants. The Inuit eat blueberries, cranberries, and crowberries, while the caribou feast on reindeer lichen.

Nunavut is home to about half the world's polar bears. They feed on the ringed seals that live in the area. Caribou are also abundant, with

Nunavut grows two varieties of cranberry. These are the bog cranberry, and the lingonberry.

more than 750,000 living in the territory. The Arctic waters are home to beluga whales, narwhals, and **bowheads**. Seals and walruses are common Nunavut residents. Hares, squirrels, foxes, weasels, and wolves also make their homes in the area.

Only a few birds survive on the cold tundra. Snowy owls, eider ducks, and gyrfalcons brave the elements and are permanent residents of the territory. Many seabirds will also come north in the spring and summer to breed on the rocky coasts. There is a delicate balance in these barren lands, and each plant and animal plays an important role in the food chain to keep the **ecosystem** strong.

The male narwhal's horn is actually a tooth and can grow up to 2.7 m long.

The Arctic hare generally lives in treeless areas, north of the treeline in the tundra of Nunavut.

Every summer, cruise ships travel the seas of Nunavut.

TOURISM

Many people travel to Nunavut to take in its unique scenery. Wilderness canoe trips down the Thelon River allow visitors close-up views of muskox, caribou, white arctic wolves, golden eagles, rough-legged hawks, and owls. Tourists can marvel at the spectacular wilderness, mountain fortresses, and fascinating wildlife of Auyuittuq National Park Reserve and Ellesmere Island National Park Reserve.

In summer, visitors can venture to the floe edge, where the ice meets the open sea. Here, they can see the shrimp that come to eat plankton, and the seals and whales that feed on the

Quttinirpaaq National Park on Ellesmere Island is Nunavut's largest national park. In the summer, visitors experience 24 hours of sunlight each day.

shrimp. There may even be polar bears lurking close by.

Visitor centres in various communities have demonstrations of everyday activities that took place in traditional Inuit summer camps. Others interpret the traditions of 1,000 years of Inuit life in Nunavut. The Nunatta Sunakkutaangit Museum in Iqaluit has displays that explain the history of south Baffin Island. It also exhibits a variety of Inuit art and clothing.

Tourism brings about **$30 million** into Nunavut's economy every year.

INDUSTRY

🏛 Iqaliut has expanded greatly since becoming the capital of Nunavut, with a $300 million airport in the works.

Once the new government of Nunavut took power, office buildings and houses were needed to accommodate the people employed. The construction industry continues to grow because of the business that self-government has generated. Houses are also needed because Inuit continue to move to where the jobs are being created.

The sale of Inuit art is an important industry in Nunavut. A large part of the territory's economy is based on exporting this art to other places around the world. Until the 1940s, Inuit art was almost completely unavailable to those outside the Arctic. Through marketing projects, the popularity and demand for Inuit art spread all over the world. Today, a large number of Inuit artists earn their living by selling their work.

🏛 Inuit art includes sculpture, stone work, and designs. It commonly draws from the natural landscape, using the figures of humans, animals, and landmarks.

🪧 Food is often delivered to Nunavut communities by boat.

GOODS AND SERVICES

Almost no goods are produced for sale in Nunavut. Many items have to be imported from the south, which makes them very expensive. For example, imported foods cost about one-third more than they do in southern Canada, due to the added shipping costs. In more remote communities, such as Grise Fiord, costs are even higher. For this reason, locally caught fish and **game** are very important. Food that is caught locally and eaten traditionally is called country food. It makes up more than half of what is eaten in Nunavut.

The governments of Canada and Nunavut are the biggest employers in the territory. The treaty that made Nunavut a territory states that 85 percent of government workers are to be Inuit. The treaty also says that Inuit companies must have increased participation in government contracts. The government hires private companies to build office complexes. Other companies provide services, including retail stores and taxis, to accommodate the needs of government employees and other residents.

🪧 There are no roads to Nunavut, so people often travel there by plane.

Health care services in Nunavut are provided by the government. There is one hospital in Iqaluit and about 14 community health centres throughout Nunavut's regions. These centres offer nursing, children's welfare, and counselling services.

About 5 percent of government employees work in education, which is also managed directly in the regions. All communities have schools, and the main community college in Nunavut is the Arctic College in Iqaluit. The institute provides guidance in traditional knowledge, science, research, and technology. To maintain Inuit traditions and ways of life, the government is developing an Inuktituk curriculum and training Inuit teachers. Providing classes in Inuktituk is necessary because it is the working language of the government.

Nunavut Arctic College has five campuses located throughout the territory.

ABORIGINAL PEOPLES

The pre-Dorset people arrived in the Canadian Arctic about 4,500 years ago. They are believed to have been the descendants of the first Palaeoeskimos in North America. These people formed small groups to follow the caribou and seal, and they used tools and weapons made of flint and bone. They lived in tents made of animal skin.

The Dorset people emerged about 2,500 years ago. In the spring, they hunted walruses, caribou, small mammals, and seals. They caught fish in the summer and trapped seals in the fall and winter. Some of the food they caught was stored in **caches** for the long winter seasons.

Nunavut's present-day Inuit are descended from the Thule, who originally migrated from Alaska. The summer homes of the Thule were tents made of animal skins, but their winter homes were solid structures. The Thule's winter homes were sunk into the ground. They had a stone floor, a whale bone or stone frame, and a roof of sealskin. Houses were covered with sod and heated by seal

The Thule used movable tents in the summer. They constructed more permanent underground homes in the winter.

Nunavut has **four official languages**, two of which, Inuinnaqtun and Inuktitut, are **native**.

or whale oil burned in a stone lamp. The Thule's graves consisted of piles of stones, with the remains of the person and their belongings placed nearby.

The Thule hunted game with bows and arrows or spears. In summer, they hunted whales from kayaks and fished with **tridents** and hooks. The Thule brought with them their expertise in marine hunting. Having developed techniques in the Bering Sea, the Thule hunted marine animals as large as bowhead whales. They ate the meat and used the bones to support their winter homes.

The Inuit made warm clothing from caribou and seal skins.

EXPLORERS

🧍 Sir Martin Frobisher encountered Inuit on his search for the Northwest Passage.

The first European to reach Nunavut was an English explorer named Sir Martin Frobisher. He sailed west from the Atlantic Ocean in search of the **Northwest Passage**. In 1576, he landed on Baffin Island and named the area Frobisher Strait. He returned to the area two more times in search of gold.

The search for the Northwest Passage brought many other explorers to the area. In the 1580s, John Davis tried his luck at finding the passage, but ice floes blocked his route. In 1610, Henry Hudson believed he had succeeded in finding the Northwest Passage when he entered the bay now named for him. His ship became iced in, and the cold climate led to an angry crew. His crew **mutinied**, and Hudson and several others were set adrift in a small boat. They were never seen again.

John Franklin has been credited with laying the groundwork for the discovery of the Northwest Passage. Franklin made two trips to northern

🧍 In 2014, one of Franklin's ships, the HMS *Erebus*, was found in the waters off King William Island.

Canada. These trips helped pave the way for the exploration of Canada's northern lands. Franklin explored and mapped much of the Far North. These efforts eventually assisted in the discovery of the Northwest Passage.

In 1845, Franklin set out with 129 British navy sailors. His ships became stuck in ice, and the crews were lost when they left the ships. The British Navy mapped most of the Arctic islands and straits while searching for Franklin and his crew. They were later found to have died in the freezing and difficult conditions.

Roald Amundsen is well known around the world, but he is especially important to Canadian history. On a voyage lasting from 1903 to 1906, he became the first person to navigate the Northwest Passage. Amundsen was the first

Roald Amundsen was 34 years old when he completed his Northwest Passage journey.

to finally conquer the freezing temperatures and massive icebergs of the Arctic water and sail over the northernmost point of North America. In doing so, he realized the dreams of centuries of explorers and captured the imaginations of people around the world.

It took European explorers more than 300 years, and many disastrous expeditions, to finally find the Northwest Passage.

The Inuit played important roles as guides, hunters, and interpreters for European settlers.

EARLY SETTLERS

Basque and Portuguese people came to Nunavut in the 1500s for fish and whales, but they did not settle there. Whalers continued to come for four centuries in search of whale oil and baleen. Whale oil was used in European and North American lamps, and baleen, the bony plates from the whale, did many of the jobs that plastic does today.

By the 1850s, whalers had established whaling stations. This changed some traditional Inuit ways. Many Inuit began to stay and work with the whalers instead of going inland in the summer to hunt. The Inuit did most of the whaling and traded oil for guns, metal pots, cloth, utensils, and alcohol. Contact with Europeans had a price, however. Many Inuit died from diseases brought by Europeans.

Missionaries followed the whalers and traders to the eastern Arctic. It was their aim to convert the Inuit from their belief in **shamans** to Christianity. According to traditional Inuit belief, shamans are men or women who bring health and prosperity and know the secrets of magic and religion.

As whaling declined, the fur trade between Inuit and Europeans became more common.

Stretching Polar Bear's Skin.

Reverend Edmund Peck set up the first mission in 1894 on Black Lead Island near Pangnirtung in the Cumberland Sound. He helped develop a written form of Inuktitut using symbols. He then translated the Bible into this script. The Inuit called Reverend Peck "Uqammak," which means "the one who speaks well." The script he developed is still used today.

Other missionaries travelled to Inuit camps spreading the word of Christianity and discouraging the use of shamans. The Inuit adopted many aspects of Christianity, and sometimes they mixed various religious ideas. At the same time, they lost many of their traditional beliefs. Inuit names were hard for missionaries to pronounce, so they gave the Inuit biblical names. The government simply gave them numbers stamped on a disc and looped around their necks.

Churches set up the first schools and hospitals. During the 1920s and 1930s, five **residential** schools were established. Children as young as five were taken away from their own communities to learn the Christian way of life. Education by the missionaries continued until the 1960s when the government began to build schools.

Today, Inuit communities must register to hunt bowhead whales. They usually can harvest one per year.

⚲ Igloos, or snowhouses, are built from the bottom in a spiral. The structure is supported by the key block at the top of the dome.

CULTURAL GROUPS

The Inuit way of life stems from an ancient society in which survival depended both on teamwork and on respect for one's natural surroundings. Today, the Inuit in Nunavut continue to respect their environment and to believe in the importance of sharing. The sharing of game and fish among families is still a vital part of Inuit society. Many Inuit believe that food tastes better when it is shared with family and friends.

Food in Nunavut is very different from most Canadian dishes. Among the most popular foods are arctic char, caribou, and muskox, which tastes like beef. Raw seal is a traditional dish. Other favourites include maktaaq, which consists of the outer skin of the whale served raw, and dips such as aalu, which is made up of caribou or seal meat, fat, blood, and ptarmigan intestines. Misiraq, which is aged seal blubber,

⚲ Some people believe maktaaq tastes like coconut. Others say it tastes like fried egg.

and nirukkaq, which are the contents of a caribou's stomach, are other unique dips.

Inuktitut is spoken throughout Nunavut, but dialects and accents vary from region to region. In Kitikmeot, or western Nunavut, the name of the Inuit language is Inuinnaqtun. A large portion of the Inuit population in Nunavut speaks English, but Inuit strive to keep their traditional language alive. They have also added new words to their vocabulary, some of which are related to the English word. For example, when European explorers arrived, the Inuit were introduced to sugar and paper. They adopted these words into their own language, and now *sukaq* and *paipaaq* are Inuktitut words.

Older generations of Inuit pass on not only their hunting expertise, but their storing and cooking knowledge as well.

Snowmobiles, rifles, schools, and permanent housing have had a great influence on the Inuit. Although older Inuit speak only Inuktituk, most younger adults are comfortable in both the Inuit and mainstream Canadian worlds. More and more, young people are taking advantage of modern technology, including the internet.

About 80 percent of Inuit report sharing their country food with other households in their close-knit communities.

The traditional Inuit drum is made from caribou skin stretched over softened driftwood.

ARTS AND ENTERTAINMENT

Art is a valued part of Inuit life. It ranges from sculpture and fabric-making to art prints and jewellery. The Inuit carve in soapstone, **serpentine**, marble, ivory, and bone. Early sculptures usually represented local activities, mythical figures, or the shapes and spirits of animals. Printmaking, which is a growing Inuit art form, also tells stories of wilderness survival, traditional myths, and shamans.

Another traditional art form among the Inuit is storytelling. Much of Inuit history is preserved through this favourite pastime. At celebrations, people tell stories with important themes and messages, or stories that detail the hardships of hunting. Celebrations also involve singing, drumming, and plenty of food.

Music has always been an important part of Inuit life. For centuries, drum dancing has welcomed visitors and celebrated births, weddings, deaths, and successful hunts. Singers, usually women, would sit in a circle while drummers played. Men would volunteer to dance in the circle. Drum dancing is now performed mainly for tourists and on ceremonial occasions.

Traditional **throat singing** is a competitive **game.** The first person to **laugh** loses.

Susan Aglukark has had a remarkable career, performing for audiences such as Queen Elizabeth and Nelson Mandela.

Another form of Inuit music is throat singing. It involves two or three singers, usually women. They stand face to face making rhythmic noises by breathing out from the throat. The sound resonating between the singers often represents the sounds of birds or animals.

Some of Nunavut's musicians have earned acclaim beyond the territory. Arviat's Susan Aglukark has won fame all over Canada by mixing Inuit chants with pop music in English and Inuktituk. Her songs discuss the discrimination against Inuit peoples and her own personal tragedies and successes. They also touch on Inuit rituals and values, and the hardships of northern life. Aglukark has won an Aboriginal Achievement Award and a Juno Award for best new solo artist. The throat singing duo, Tudjaat, has appeared in concert and on record with Susan Aglukark.

🏠 Inuit art tends to have realistic details, though many Inuit artists have been exploring different forms.

The yearly Nunavut Quest Dog Sled Race is always about 500 kilometres in length.

SPORTS

Activities such as camping, kayaking, dogsledding, snowmobiling, hunting, and fishing are considered recreational sports in southern Canada. In Nunavut, they are more than that. These sports are a part of the traditional Inuit way of life. The people of Nunavut also enjoy sports such as hockey, curling, and badminton. They even enjoy a round of golf now and then.

Traditional Inuit games are both a diversion to Nunavut's long, cold months and a way to stay fit. Many of the games are based on skills that were once needed to survive in the Arctic. One of the most popular games is the high kick. Among the types of high kicks are the two-

foot and one-foot high kicks, and the Alaskan high kick. The one- and two-foot high kicks involve jumping up, kicking an object that is suspended in the air, and landing in a certain way. The Alaskan high kick requires great skill and wrist strength, as part of the kick involves balancing the entire body on one wrist.

Long winters and heavy snow and ice mean that hockey can be played almost anywhere in Nunavut.

Toonik Tyme is Nunavut's largest festival of traditional Inuit games. It takes place in Iqaluit every spring. Igloo building, snowmobile and dog-team races, entertainment, and feasting are all a part of the fun.

Other athletic competitions are held throughout the territory. The Midnight Sun Marathon celebrates the longest day of the year, attracting runners from all over the world. One hundred runners from Canada, the United States, Europe, and Australia are invited to run in the 10-km, 32-km, 42-km, or 84-km races between Arctic Bay and Nanisivik. The Midnight Sun Golf Tournament at Pelly Bay is played on a homemade course. Golfers tee off on rugs lent by local families.

The Kitikmeot Northern Games are held in the summer. Events include Good Man and Good Woman contests in family skills. These skills include tea boiling, duck plucking, seal skinning, and **bannock** making.

In the two-foot high kick, a player must kick the object with both feet while landing on both feet as well.

How to Improve My Community

Strong communities make strong provinces. Think about what features are important in your community. What do you value? Education? Health? Forests? Safety? Beautiful spaces? Government works to help citizens create ideal living conditions that are fair to all by providing services in communities. Consider what changes you could make in your community. How would they improve your province as a whole? Using this concept web as a guide, write a report that outlines the features you think are most important in your community and what improvements could be made. A strong province needs strong communities.

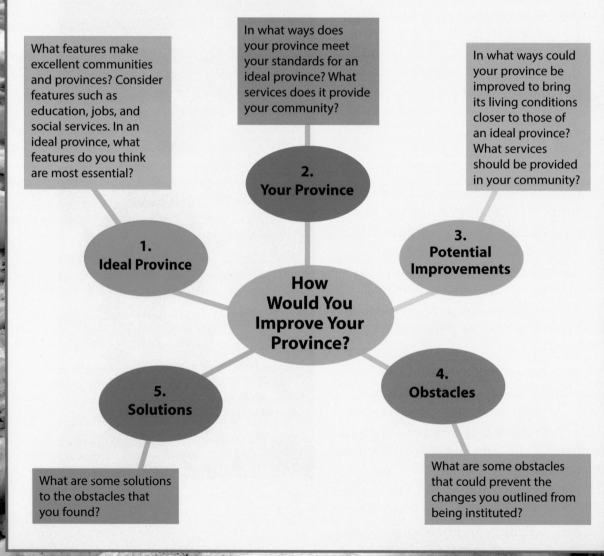

What features make excellent communities and provinces? Consider features such as education, jobs, and social services. In an ideal province, what features do you think are most essential?

In what ways does your province meet your standards for an ideal province? What services does it provide your community?

In what ways could your province be improved to bring its living conditions closer to those of an ideal province? What services should be provided in your community?

2.
Your Province

1.
Ideal Province

3.
Potential
Improvements

How
Would You
Improve Your
Province?

5.
Solutions

4.
Obstacles

What are some solutions to the obstacles that you found?

What are some obstacles that could prevent the changes you outlined from being instituted?

BRAIN TEASERS

Test your knowledge of Nunavut by trying to answer these brain teasers. The answers are printed upside down underneath each question.

1 What is the capital city of Nunavut?

Iqaluit

2 What does Nunavut mean?

Inuktitut for "our land"

3 What do the colours blue, white, and gold represent on Nunavut's official flag?

Sea, land, and sky

4 Where are Nunavut's two largest lakes?

Baffin Island

5 Who are the largest employers in Nunavut?

The governments of Canada and Nunavut

6 What culture lived in the Nunavut area before the Inuit?

The Dorset culture

7 What were explorers such as Sir John Franklin and Roald Amundsen looking for in Nunavut?

The Northwest Passage

8 What is country food?

Traditional food caught in Nunavut

Key Words

bannock: a traditional flatbread

bowheads: a type of whale with a very large head and a lower lip that curves up in a bow on each side

caches: places for storing supplies

Canadian Shield: a region of ancient rock that encircles Hudson Bay and covers a large portion of Canada's mainland

dialect: form of speech characteristic to a certain region

ecosystem: the relationship between organisms and their environment

fjords: long, deep, and narrow sea inlets formed by glaciers

game: animals that are hunted for sport

inukshuk: a stone used by the Inuit to mark a location

muskeg: an area of swamp or marsh

mutinied: to have rebelled against an authority

narwhal: a whale that swims in the Arctic seas; males have a huge tusk that extends from a tooth in the upper jaw

Northwest Passage: a short-cut route for ships from the Atlantic to the Pacific Ocean

pure breeds: animals bred from parents of the same breed

residential: designed for people to live in

serpentine: a green or spotted mineral resembling a serpent's skin

shamans: men or women believed to have spiritual powers

tridents: spears that have three prongs

tundra: an Arctic or subarctic plain with a permanently frozen subsoil

Index